Using this book

This book is made up from three booklets, each one separately stapled. Pull out the centre booklet first. This contains Tests B and C. Next pull out the booklet containing Test A and the child's answer sheet for the Mental Arithmetic Test. The remaining booklet has background information, test answers/helpful tips, the Mental Arithmetic Test and conversion information for changing your child's test scores into National Curriculum Levels.

Taking the tests

Before you set the test
It is important that your child feels comfortable about sitting these practice papers. Explain that they should help him or her to become used to the kinds of activities in the actual tests.

At the start
Your child should take Test A first, then Test B and finally the Mental Arithmetic Test. Test C should only be attempted if your child scores a combined mark of 100 or more on the three main tests. Do each test on a separate day, at a time when your child is not tired or irritable, and in a quiet place with no distractions. Make sure you allow plenty of time for taking, marking and talking afterwards about the test. Be as positive as you can so that your child starts each test confidently. It is important he or she should not feel over-anxious or pressured. If your child shows any signs of distress, leave the test until a later date. Finally, read the instructions together carefully and ensure your child understands them.

During the test
How rigidly you observe the time-limits for these practice tests depends on how far you wish to replicate the actual test conditions. You may wish to insist on your child working entirely alone, asking no questions. Or you may prefer not to put your child under the pressure of keeping strictly to 'test conditions'. Working through practice papers is a perfectly valid test preparation activity. You could help your child increase speed by giving extra practice later. As with any skill, the more practice you have, the more efficient you become.

For Tests A, B and C, make sure he or she has a pencil, ruler and a clock or watch for timing the test. For Tests B and C, your child will also need a protractor and may use a calculator. For the Mental Arithmetic Test, the instructions can be found on page 12 of this booklet.

Once your child has started, don't fuss and keep looking over his or her shoulder. If your child finishes before the end of the test time, encourage him or her to go back and check answers. If your child does not finish before the time is up, stop the test, make a note of where your child is up to, then allow your child to finish the test, if he or she wishes. However, only that part of the test finished during the allowed time should be marked for the final test score.

Marking the answers

Mark all the tests with your child present. If your child gets an answer, wrong go over the question and try to discover how the mistake was made. If he or she did not attempt the question at all, discuss the problem and see if you can elicit a correct answer by phrasing the question differently. The important thing is to try to encourage children to 'think' for themselves. Don't just tell your child the answers. This is of no benefit at all.

Marking Tests A, B and C
Use the mark schemes provided on pages 5–11 to award marks as indicated. The arrangement of the answers is fairly clear, but you may have to use your discretion occasionally!

● In the margin of each test paper, there is a mark box alongside each question part. Write the number of marks scored by your child for that part of the question in this box. If your child gets the question wrong, put '0' in the box. If your child does not attempt the question, put a '–' in the box. Do not leave any mark box empty.

● At the bottom of all the right-hand page margins is a 'total' box for the number of marks scored on that double (or single) page. Write each of these totals on to the 'marking grid' on the front cover of the test booklet and add them up.

● Transfer the final total mark to the correct text column of the first table on the inside back cover of this booklet.

Marking the Mental Arithmetic Test

The mark scheme for the Mental Arithmetic Test is on page 11 of this booklet. In the mark boxes, write either '1' for a correct response or '0' for an incorrect response. Total up the marks and write the score in the space provided on your child's answer sheet. Then transfer this mark to the correct test column on the first table on the inside back cover of this booklet.

Using the 'Tips to help your child'

Each answer page for Tests A and B includes suggestions for ways in which you can help to improve your child's test performance if you find that he or she is having particular difficulty with either a specific area of the maths curriculum or a specific question type. You may, of course, have some ideas of your own on how to help your child. If you do so, always beware of causing confusion if any 'help' is different from what your child has been taught in school.

What do National Curriculum Levels mean?

For children between the ages of 5 and 14 the National Curriculum is divided into eight levels of attainment. Children are expected to advance approximately one level for every two years they are at school. At the end of Key Stage 1, children are expected to be working at Level 2. By the end of Key Stage 2, it is expected they will be at Level 4. The table shows you at what level an average child should be working for each of the six years of primary school.

Key Stage	Year	NC Level
1	1	1
1	2	2
2	3	2/3
2	4	3
2	5	3/4
2	6	4/5

The questions in Tests A and B and the Mental Arithmetic Test in this book cater for children working at NC Levels 2–5. Extension Test C caters for children working at NC Level 6, but should only be taken by your child if he or she scores a combined mark of 100 or more in the three main tests. After you have marked the test papers in this book, follow the instructions on the inside back cover to work out your child's National Curriculum Level.

Important note

In marking National Test papers, external markers use their professional judgement, based on years of experience. It is not to be expected that as a parent you will be able to bring the same experience and judgement to marking these practice papers. The marks you award and the level your child gains as a result of doing these practice papers may therefore differ from those that examiners or teachers at your child's school would give. Please remember too that the purpose of this book is to provide test practice for your child, as well as to highlight any areas of difficulty he or she may be having. We suggest that you use the information about your child's performance in these practice papers as a basis for discussion with your child's teacher, who will be able to offer advice and ideas for helping your child to improve in areas of need.

Tips to help your child – Test A

| Q | | MARKS |

1. Award 1 mark each for a and b (do not credit a mark if the £ sign is missing). **2**
a. £1.76
b. £20.64

This question concentrates on skills associated with adding and subtracting amounts of money. Help your child to improve his or her confidence in this area of maths through practical work with coins – for example, adding up a total cost or checking the change given.

2. Award 1 mark each for a and b. **2**
7.50
1.30

Give your child frequent practice in reading and writing times, using both the 12-hour and the 24-hour clock systems.

3. Award 1 mark if all the following five numbers are circled: **1**
40, 270, 520, 150, 110.

Point out that answers to the 10 times table always end in 0. Work with your child to try and discover useful patterns in the other tables – for example, the times tables for even numbers contain only even numbers, while those for odd numbers contain both odd and even numbers. Practise all times tables up to 10 × 10.

4. Award 1 mark if all the coins except the 1p and one 5p are crossed out. **1**

If possible, let your child pay for some items in shops by choosing the correct coins to make up a given amount.

5. Award 1 mark if all three stages are written in the box in the correct order (credit the mark if stages 1 and 2 are the other way round, but stage 3 must be last). **1**
6 + 8 = 14
20 + 40 = 60
14 + 60 = 74

Write out some more two-digit addition sums and ask your child to work them out using the same method as in this question. Then see whether your child can add three two-digit numbers using the same method.

6. Award 1 mark each for a–c. **3**
a. Credit the mark only if all three columns of the bar graph are correctly shaded.

If your child finds this question difficult, show him or her how to transfer the information from the table to the bar graph. Then change the amounts in the 'Number of children' column on the table, and ask your child to transfer this new information to a newly-drawn bar graph. You may find it useful to extend the 'y' axis of the graph from 20 to 50, allowing a wider range of numbers to be represented. Now question your child orally about the information shown on the new graph, using questions similar to those found in parts b and c of question 6.

b. bananas
c. 5 (five)

7. Award 1 mark if both answers are correct. **1**
32   26

Make up some more 'function machine' questions to give to your child, using all four mathematical operations (+, –, × and ÷) in the centre boxes. Start with easy questions to establish the principle.

8. Award 1 mark each for a–c. **3**
a. square
b. triangle
c. rectangle **or** oblong (credit either answer)

Your child should be familiar with the names and properties of all the following plane (two-dimensional) shapes: square, rectangle, triangle, circle, pentagon, hexagon, octagon and parallelogram. He or she should be able to identify each of these shapes from a written or oral description of its key features.

9. Award 1 mark if all answers are correct (do not credit an answer with the £ sign missing). **1**
£1.96   £3.04
£2.55   £5.70

When your child is writing amounts of money, make sure he or she is aware of the rule that the pound sign (£) and the pence symbol (p) are never used together – for example, you can write £2.49 or 249p, but **not** £2.49p. Give your child opportunities to practise using this rule.

10. Award 1 mark for a correct answer. **1**
38

Make up some 'real life' two-digit subtraction problems for your child to solve, responding either orally or in written form (as he or she chooses).

| Q | Answers | MARKS | Tips |

11. Award 1 mark for a correct answer. **1**
All four measurements must be correct to gain a mark (credit answers with no units shown).
130mm 165mm 195mm 230mm

Conversion of measures is an important aspect of National Curriculum mathematics. Try to make sure that your child can change millimetres to centimetres, centimetres to metres and metres to kilometres (as well as grams to kilograms and millilitres to litres).

12. Award 1 mark each for a–d (credit names spelt incorrectly). **4**
a. Nicholas
b. Helen
c. 26 min
d. Alexandra

This question is about interpreting data displayed in table form. You could reinforce the skills needed to tackle this type of problem by asking your child to make up a table of numerical data. For instance, he or she could keep a record of how much TV (in different categories) each member of the family watches. Follow this up by asking your child questions about the information on his or her table.

13. Award 1 mark each for a and b. **2**
a. 1200 metres (credit a correct answer with the units missing)
b. 120

Your child should approach questions of this kind in a calm and methodical way, first working out exactly what the question is asking and then developing a strategy to find the answer. Look for the steps that your child has used in his or her working out.

14. Award one mark. **1**

| 6 hours | 29 minutes |

A local bus or train timetable will provide opportunities for you and your child to practise time difference calculations involving periods of less than an hour. National and international timetables can be used for more difficult time difference problems.

15. Award 1 mark each for a–c. **3**
a. The following amounts should be crossed out:
0.49 $\frac{4}{10}$ 0.27   45%

b.

| | 1 | 8 | 0 | 0 |

c. 7051   7105   7150   7501   7510

This question requires your child to understand the comparative values of fractional, decimal and percentage amounts. Many good primary maths textbooks are available to help your child with problems of this kind. Point out that subtracting the known number in the sum from the answer will give the number required in part b. Give your child some groups of four-digit, five-digit and six-digit numbers to order by size.

16. Award 1 mark for a correct answer: **1**
half an hour (accept $\frac{1}{2}$ an hour or 30 minutes).

Use the distance-time graph to ask your child more questions about the journey. For example, you could ask how far the coach travelled between 11.00 am and 11.45 am (50km), or how far it travelled altogether (150km).

17. Award 1 mark each for a–c. **3**
a. All four numbers must be circled to gain the mark (if any wrong numbers are circled as well as the correct ones, then mark the answer wrong).

33	40	(66)	57
65	(54)	58	(42)
(24)	49	11	26

b. Award 1 mark if both answers are correct.
4725
69 248
c. 30

Point out to your child that numbers in the 6 times table always end in an even number, and therefore any odd numbers in the list can be ignored. Ask him or her to divide by 6 the eight numbers from the question that are **not** multiples of six, and to write down the answers with their remainders. Then ask him or her to change the remainders into fractional amounts (in their lowest terms) – for example, 5 r 3 would become $\frac{33}{6}$ or $5\frac{1}{2}$.
    Write out a further list of numbers for your child to add together as in part b of question 17. Reverse the process by giving your child some 'ready-made' numbers and asking him or her to partition them – for example: 4327 = 4000 + 300 + 20 + 7.
    Invent some problems similar to part c of question 17, where a remainder is ignored.

18. Award 1 mark each for a–c. **3**
a. E
b. K
c. H

Remind your child that the horizontal co-ordinate is always given before the vertical co-ordinate. Playing the game 'Battleships' is an enjoyable way of helping your child to master the use of co-ordinates. Also, make sure that he or she is familiar with the four points of the compass. Discuss the relative positions and locations of objects with your child when you are outdoors.

MATHS
Practice for Key Stage 2 National tests
ges 10-11

Test A Booklet

CALCULATOR NOT ALLOWED
For this test you will need a **pencil**, a **ruler** and a **watch** or **clock** to time yourself.
Sit at a table in a quiet place.

Ask an adult to read through the test instructions with you before you start.

INSTRUCTIONS

1. You will have **45 minutes** to do this test.
2. Work as quickly and as carefully as possible.
3. Do not worry if you cannot finish all the questions. Do as many as you can.
4. If you wish to change an answer, cross it out and write your new answer next to it.
5. Do not waste time on a question you cannot do. Move quickly on to the next one.
6. Read the instructions carefully and write your answers in the spaces highlighted by the pencil symbol.
7. Some pages have 'working out areas'. Use these spaces for doing your working out. If you need to do further working out, use any other empty space on the page.
8. Move straight on from one page to the next without waiting to be told.
9. Once you have started the test, you must not talk to anyone or ask any questions.
10. If there is time left when you have finished, check your answers and try to do any questions you missed out earlier.

First Name

Last Name

MARKING GRID

Page	Marks possible	Marks scored
2–3	7	
4–5	7	
6–7	7	
8–9	7	
10–11	9	
12–13	6	
14–15	7	
TOTAL	50	

Let's learn at home
MATHS

1. Here are the prices of some common items.

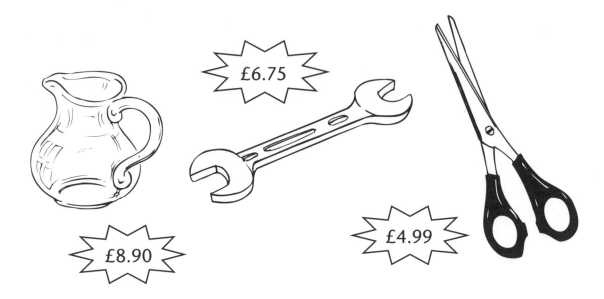

£6.75

£8.90

£4.99

a. Find the difference in cost between the scissors and the spanner.

1a

1 mark

b. Find the total cost of all three items.

WORKING OUT AREA

1b

1 mark

2. Write these times in the same way as the one that has been done for you.

a.

b.

2a

1 mark

2b

1 mark

3.25

3. Circle the numbers that are in the ten times table.

40   270   520   502

91   150   101   110   75

3

1 mark

4. Put a cross through the coins you need to make £3.67.

4

1 mark

Add 26 and 48 using Ruth's method. Show the three stages.

5. Here is a way used by Ruth to add 47 and 38:

7 + 8 = 15

40 + 30 = 70

15 + 70 = 85

5

1 mark

TOTAL

3

6. Some children were asked which fruit they liked the most. Here are the results:

Fruit	Number of children
Oranges	10
Bananas	20
Apples	15

a. Fill in the results on this bar graph.

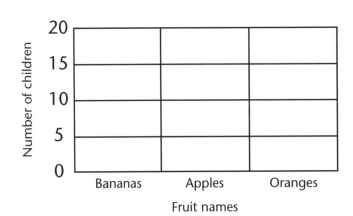

6a

1 mark

b. Which fruit was twice as popular as oranges?

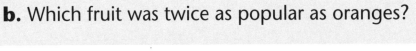

6b

1 mark

c. How many more children liked bananas most than liked apples most?

6c

1 mark

WORKING
OUT AREA

7. Work out the missing numbers in these function machines.

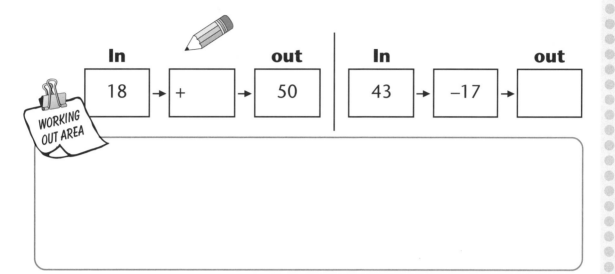

In		out	In		out
18	→ + →	50	43	→ −17 →	

WORKING OUT AREA

8. Helen has thought of three clues, each of which describes a **2-D** shape.

I know what to say!

Read her clues and work out what each shape is.

a. 'This shape has four equal sides and four right angles.'

It must be a _____

b. 'This shape has three sides.'

It must be a _____

c. 'This shape has four right angles with sides that are not all the same length.'

It must be a _____

Let's learn at home
MATHS

Test A
Booklet

7

1 mark

8a

1 mark

8b

1 mark

8c

1 mark

TOTAL

9. 237p can be shown as £2.37.

Show these amounts in the same way.

196p [   ]   304p [   ]

255p [   ]   570p [   ]

9

1 mark

10. Thomas has 55 computer games. He sells 17.
How many computer games will Thomas have left?

WORKING
OUT AREA

10

1 mark

11. Write in **mm** the measurements marked by the arrows.

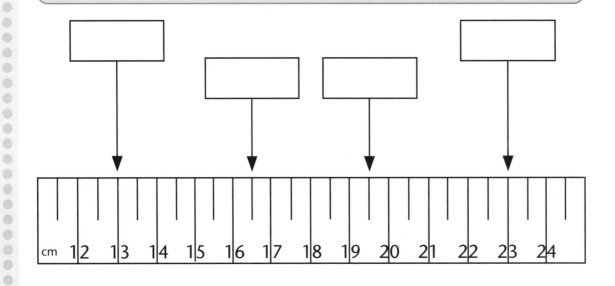

11

1 mark

6

12. The table below records the time it took four children on a sponsored walk to cover a distance of 2km.

The table also shows how long it took each child to walk 500m, 1km and 1500m on the way.

	500m	1km	1500m	2km
Colin	6 min	13 min	21 min	32 min
Helen	5 min	11 min	18 min	28 min
Nicholas	8 min	18 min	28 min	36 min
Alexandra	9 min	16 min	27 min	40 min

a. Who took the longest time to reach 1500m?

12a

1 mark

b. Which child walked the first kilometre the fastest?

12b

1 mark

c. How long did it take Colin to walk the final 1500m?

12c

1 mark

d. Who was the slowest during the first quarter of the walk?

12d

1 mark

TOTAL

13. The string in this ball is 25 metres long.

Balls of string can be bought in boxes of eight.

a. What is the total length of string in six boxes?

13a

1 mark

b. How many balls of string are there in 15 boxes?

13b

1 mark

WORKING
OUT AREA

14. A train leaves London at 23.46 on Friday.
It arrives in Glasgow at 06.15 on the following day.

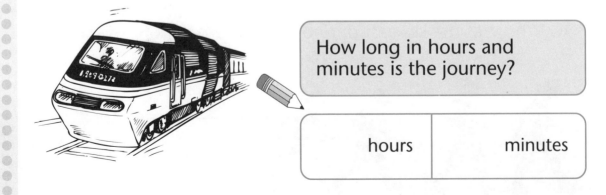

How long in hours and
minutes is the journey?

| hours | minutes |

14

1 mark

8

MATHS
Practice for
Key Stage 2
National tests

ges 10-11

Let's learn at home

MATHS

Test B Booklet

CALCULATOR ALLOWED

For this test you will need a **pencil**, a **ruler**, a **protractor** and a **watch** or **clock** to time yourself. You may also have a **calculator** if you wish. Sit at a table in a quiet place.

Ask an adult to read through the test instructions with you before you start.

INSTRUCTIONS

1. You will have **45 minutes** to do this test.
2. Work as quickly and as carefully as possible.
3. Do not worry if you do not finish all the questions. Do as many as you can.
4. If you wish to change an answer, cross it out and write your new answer next to it.
5. Do not waste time on a question you cannot do. Move on to the next one.
6. Read the instructions carefully and write your answers in the spaces highlighted by the pencil symbol.
7. If you need to do any working out, use a 'working out area' or any empty space on the page.
8. Move straight on from one page to the next without waiting to be told.
9. Once you have started the test, you must not talk to anyone or ask any questions.
10. If there is time left when you have finished, check your answers and try to do any questions you missed out earlier.

First Name

Last Name

1. Fill in the missing numbers to make each sum balance.

a. 47p + [ ] = 95p

b. £179 × 2 = [ ]

123g – 58g = [ ]

[ ] ÷ 4 = £17

WORKING
OUT AREA

1a

1 mark

1b

1 mark

2. AB is a mirror line. Draw the triangle after its reflection in AB.

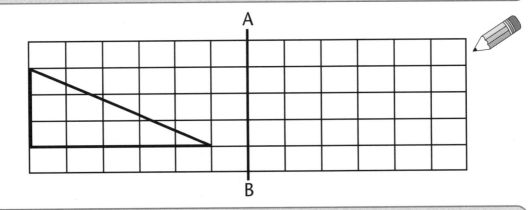

2

1 mark

3. Fill in each digital watch face with the time shown below it, using the 24-hour clock.

6.35am   2.55pm

3

1 mark

4. A shop sells envelopes in packets of 36.

Nathan buys 3 packets.
Katie buys 5 packets.
Zoe buys 1 packet less than Nathan.

a. What would be the total cost of Nathan's envelopes?

4a

1 mark

b. How much more does Katie spend on envelopes than Nathan?

4b

1 mark

c. How many envelopes would there be in nine packets?

4c

1 mark

d. Divide by 3 the total number of envelopes bought by all the children.

4d

1 mark

WORKING OUT AREA

TOTAL

3

5. Six children were sorted into the sets shown on the Venn diagram.

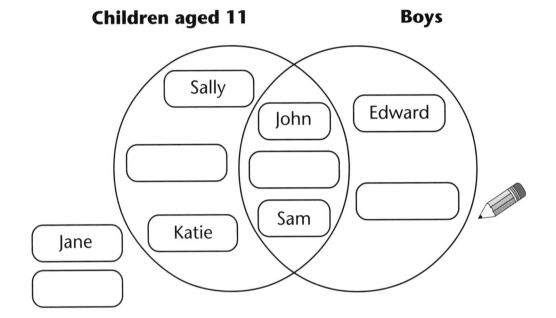

Children aged 11   **Boys**

Sally

John   Edward

Sam

Katie

Jane

a. Use the information above to fill in the table below.

Boys		Girls	
Name	Age	Name	Age
John		Sally	11
	10		11
	11		10

This is Stuart. He is 9 years old.

5a

1 mark

b. Place his name in the correct box on the Venn diagram.

5b

1 mark

This is Jenny. She is twelve years old.

5c

1 mark

c. Place her name in the correct box on the Venn diagram.

6. This magnifying glass has a mass of 350 grams.

a. Work out the total mass of 15 magnifying glasses.

grams

This building is 148 metres high.

b. How tall will a building a quarter of this height be?

metres

WORKING OUT AREA

7. Draw one line of symmetry on each of these shapes.

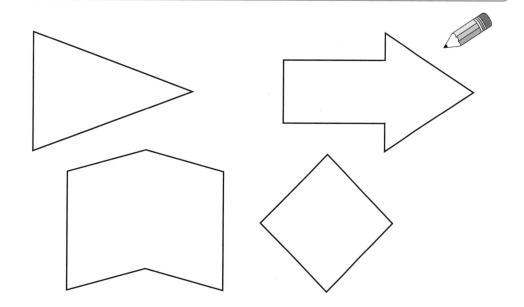

Test B Booklet

6a

1 mark

6b

1 mark

7

1 mark

TOTAL

8a. Put a different number in each rectangle so that all the numbers are in order.

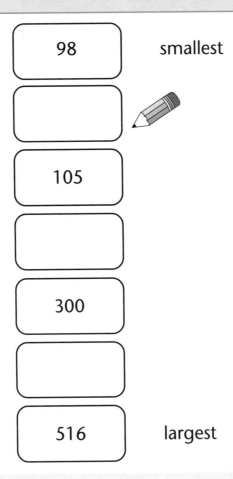

98	smallest
105	
300	
516	largest

8a

1 mark

b. Use a pencil line to connect each number to where it fits on the number line.

1 000   1 500   2 000

| 1 325 | 1 075 | 1 700 | 1 499 | 1 850 |

8b

1 mark

9. Write out three whole-number multiplication questions which all have 16 as the answer.

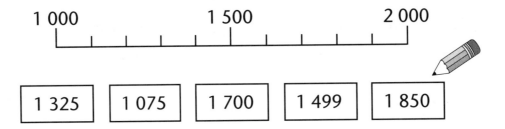

9

1 mark

6

10. This tally chart shows you how many good work awards were scored by four classes at Copp Primary School in one week.

Class 1	ЖЖ ЖЖ ЖЖ			
Class 2	ЖЖ ЖЖ ЖЖ ЖЖ				
Class 3	ЖЖ ЖЖ ЖЖ ЖЖ ЖЖ		
Class 4	ЖЖ ЖЖ ЖЖ

a. Complete this line graph to show the number of good work awards gained by each class. The line for Class 1 has been drawn for you.

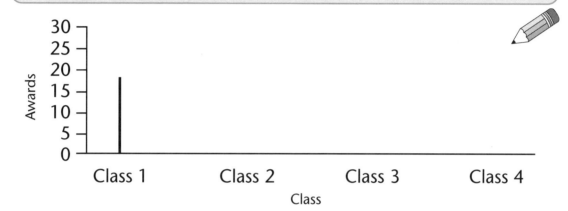

10a

1 mark

b. Which class scored the greatest number of awards?

10b

1 mark

c. Which class scored the least number of awards?

10c

1 mark

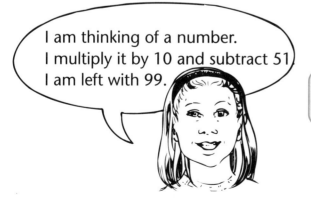

I am thinking of a number. I multiply it by 10 and subtract 51. I am left with 99.

11a. What is the number?

11a

1 mark

11b

1 mark

b. Write in the missing number. $523.6 \div \boxed{} = 23.8$

TOTAL

12a. Mark every obtuse angle in these shapes with a cross. One has been done for you.

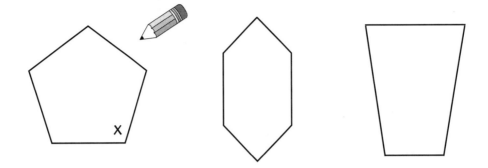

x

12a

1 mark

b. Measure the perimeter of this rectangle in centimetres.

12b

1 mark

cm

13a. Write what the three missing digits could be.

13a

1 mark

☐ ☐   × 4 =   9 ☐

b. I am thinking of a number.
I divide it by 7.
My answer is 15.

13b

1 mark

What is the number I am thinking of?

8

14. 24 children timed how long it took them to walk from the swimming pool to their homes.

They have written their journey times on the chart below.

Journey time in minutes							
3	13	8	10	14	5	9	4
16	5	14	16	4	13	7	12
7	11	2	7	9	14	15	6

Use the information on this chart to complete the frequency table below.

Time in minutes	Tally	Frequency
1–4	IIII	4
5–8		
9–12	HHt	
		8

15a. Draw a pencil line to join each number to the correct box.

| between five thousand and fifty thousand |

| more than two hundred thousand |

1 490 000   105 000   3 706   34 700

| less than five thousand |

| more than fifty thousand but less than one hundred and fifty thousand |

b. 17 000 is the same as how many hundreds?

14

3 marks

15a

1 mark

15b

1 mark

TOTAL

9

16. A supermarket carried out a survey to find out which kind of fruit people liked the most.

This bar chart shows the results.

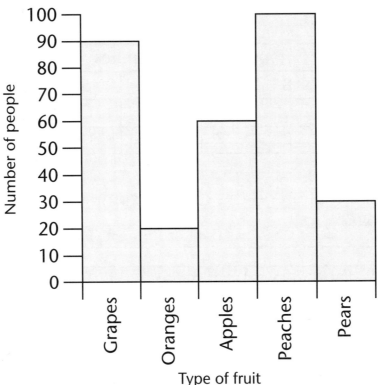

WORKING OUT AREA

16a

1 mark

a. How many people took part in the survey?

16b

1 mark

b. What fraction of the people taking part indicated peaches as their favourite fruit?

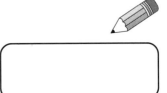

16c

1 mark

c. Which two fruits combined did 50% of the people like the best?

10

17. This chart shows the distance in miles between some large towns in Britain.

London									
503	Aberdeen								
211	445	Aberystwyth							
394	177	317	Ayr						
388	182	311	134	Berwick-upon-Tweed					
105	420	114	289	264	Birmingham				
226	308	153	180	193	123	Blackpool			
100	564	207	436	412	147	270	Bournemouth		
482	59	405	143	148	377	268	524	Braemar	
52	556	235	446	390	163	286	92	534	Brighton

a. What distance is two return journeys from Bournemouth to Ayr?

b. Calculate $\frac{3}{4}$ of the distance from Brighton to Blackpool.

18. Write in the missing digits.

a. 315 x ☐ 9 = 12 28 ☐

b. 1 ☐ 9 ☐ ÷ 6 = 216

WORKING OUT AREA

19. Change each of the amounts on the left into the units given on the right.

a. 3009m ⟶ [km]

3.04km ⟶ [m]

b. 0.49kg ⟶ [g]

2036g ⟶ [kg]

19a

1 mark

19b

1 mark

20. There are two hundred and sixteen people at an international conference. The **pie chart** below shows their nationalities.

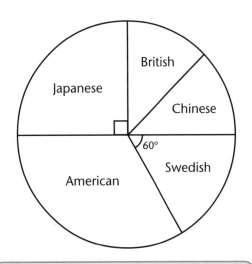

WORKING OUT AREA

a. What percentage of the people are Japanese?

[ ]

20a

1 mark

b. What fraction of the people are American?

[ ]

20b

1 mark

c. How many Swedish people are there?

[ ]

20c

1 mark

MATHS

Test B
Booklet

21. In this set of numbers, any three amounts in line **either across or down** have a total of 18.74.

3.27	12.91	2.56
6.48		8.77
8.99	2.34	7.41

a. Work out the missing number and write it in the empty space on the table.

21a

1 mark

WORKING OUT AREA

b. Choose numbers to balance this sum.

$$\boxed{} \div 10 = \boxed{4}$$

21b

1 mark

WORKING OUT AREA

c. Work out this multiplication problem.

21c

1 mark

TOTAL

$$2.83 \times 0.45 = \boxed{}$$

22. The letter **y** represents a number.

Match the expressions that mean the same. One has been done for you.

| 3 more than **y** | **y** plus **y** | **y** minus 4 |

| 3 – y | y² | 2y |

| y + 4 | y + 3 | y – 4 |

22

2 marks

23. Draw a circle around the length that is nearest to the length of a real car.

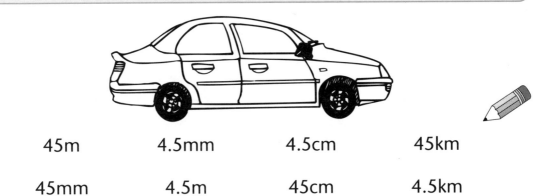

23

1 mark

| 45m | 4.5mm | 4.5cm | 45km |
| 45mm | 4.5m | 45cm | 4.5km |

24. Three 2p coins are thrown into the air.

Write down in the box all the different ways in which the coins could land. It does not matter what order the coins fall in. One possible result has been written down for you.

T, H, H

24

1 mark

TOTAL

STOP HERE

14

MARKING GRID		
Page	Marks possible	Marks scored
1	2	
2–3	12	
4–5	11	
6	5	
TOTAL	30	

Test C

CALCULATOR ALLOWED

For this test you will need a **pencil**, a **ruler**,
a **protractor** and a **watch** or **clock**.
You may also have a **calculator** if you wish.

The instructions for this test are the same as for **Test B**
except that you are only allowed **30 minutes** to
answer the questions.
Go over **Test B** instructions 2–10 again with an adult.

1. Debra and Martin went to the footwear sale.
Shoes were 10% less than their normal price.
Boots were 40% less than before the sale.

Martin bought a pair of shoes for £27.

a. What was their normal price?

1a

1 mark

Debra bought a pair of boots for £22.80.

b. What was the normal price for the boots?

1b

1 mark

WORKING OUT AREA

TOTAL

1

2. A shoe box without the flaps has a **net** as shown below.

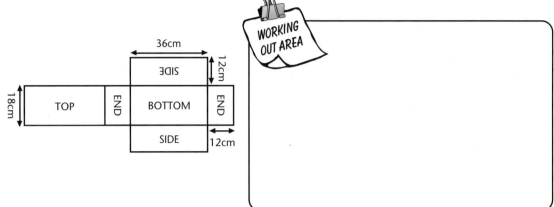

a. Work out the combined area of the top and bottom of the box in cm².

2a

1 mark

b. How much greater in cm² is the area of the top of the box than the area of one of the sides?

2b

1 mark

c. Calculate the volume of the completed box in cm³.

2c

1 mark

d. How many end pieces of the box would be needed to cover the same area as the top of the box?

2d

1 mark

e. Give the total area of the net in cm².

2e

1 mark

3. Thomas thinks of a number.
Using his calculator, he multiplies the number by itself.
He then adds 20 to the answer.
The calculator readout shows 32.96.

What was the number Thomas first thought of?
Show your working below.

Test C
Booklet

3

2 marks

WORKING
OUT AREA

4. In this diagram, which is not drawn to scale, the line AB is
parallel to the line CD.

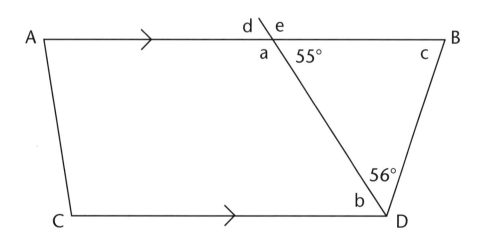

Without using a protractor, work out the values of angles a–e.

a = [   ] °   b = [   ] °   c = [   ] °

4

d = [   ] °   e = [   ] °

5 marks

TOTAL

Test C
Booklet

5

2 marks

5. Write these numbers in order of size, starting with the largest.

2.002   2.02   2.202   0.22

[   ]   [   ]   [   ]   [   ]

largest

6. This speed-time graph shows a train journey lasting an hour.

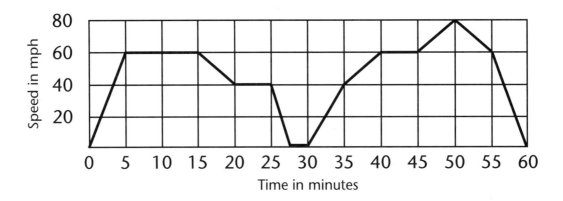

6a

1 mark

a. For how many minutes was the train travelling at 60mph?

[   ]

The train stopped once on its journey.

6b

1 mark

b. For approximately how long was the train stationary?

[   ]

6c

1 mark

c. By how much did the train slow down between the fifteenth and the twentieth minute of the trip?

[   ]

4

7. Which one of these decimals is closest in value to $\frac{1}{4}$?

0.253   0.244   0.248   0.255

7

1 mark

8. It is Wendy's turn to throw the dice. She needs a 2 or a 5 to be able to move.

What is the chance of her moving on her next turn?

8

1 mark

9. Find the value of **n** in these equations.

WORKING OUT AREA

9a

1 mark

9b

1 mark

9c

1 mark

a. $5n + 7 = 17$ $n =$

b. $8n - 3 = 21$ $n =$

c. $7n + 8 = 36$ $n =$

10. Write in the mass of the unmarked package on the scales.

1.425t   698kg   789kg

10

1 mark

TOTAL

11. Calculate the area in m² of both the shaded and unshaded parts of this pattern.

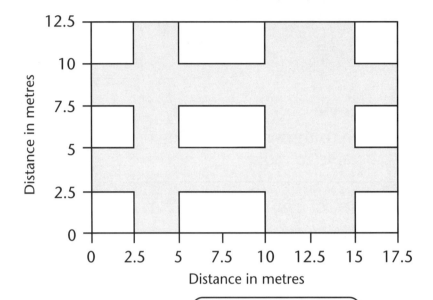

Distance in metres (y-axis): 0, 2.5, 5, 7.5, 10, 12.5

Distance in metres (x-axis): 0, 2.5, 5, 7.5, 10, 12.5, 15, 17.5

11a

1 mark

a. The shaded area equals

11b

1 mark

b. The unshaded area equals

WORKING OUT AREA

12a. £75 is divided in the ratio 4:1. How much is each part?

12a

1 mark

b. 8 torch batteries cost £8.80. What do three cost?

12b

1 mark

c. 3 men take 6 hours to lay a path. How long will it take 5 men?

12c

1 mark

TOTAL

STOP HERE

15a. Cross out each of the rectangles that shows less than a half.

| 100% | 0.49 | 0.65 | 4/10 |
| 0.27 | 45% | 3/5 | 51% |

b. Write the missing digits in the correct places in the empty box.

 [ ][ ][ ][ ][ ] + [1][0][4][0][0] = [1][2][2][0][0]

c. Write these numbers in order of size, starting with the smallest.

7501   7051   7105   7510   7150

[ ] [ ] [ ] [ ] [ ]

smallest

16. This is a graph showing a coach journey.

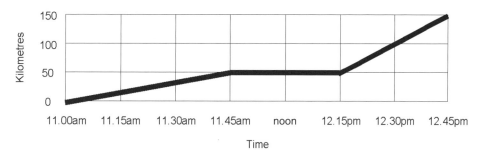

On the journey the coach broke down. How long was it stopped for?

[ ]

17a. Circle the four numbers that divide by 6 with no remainder.

33	40	66	57
65	54	58	42
24	49	11	26

17a

1 mark

b. Add these numbers together.

4000 + 20 + 5 + 700 [   ]

17b

1 mark

60 000 + 40 + 8 + 200 + 9000 [   ]

In a shop, you can buy a pack of two apples for 19p.

17c

1 mark

c. How many apples can you buy for £3? [   ]

18. Look at the grid below and answer the questions.

N
W—|—E
S

Write the letter that is:

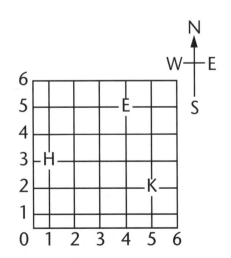

18a

1 mark

a. North of (4, 4). [   ]

18b

1 mark

b. East of (3, 2). [   ]

18c

1 mark

c. West of (6, 3). [   ]

19. The children at Susan's school are collecting money to buy some new computer software.

The chart on the right shows how much money has been collected so far.

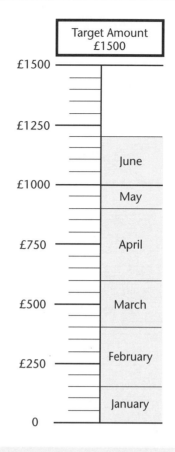

WORKING OUT AREA

a. How much more money do the children at the school need to collect in order to reach the target of £1500?

b. What is the difference between the amount of money collected in February and April and the amount collected in January and May?

Susan says,
'The chart shows that our target will be reached in one month.'

c. Use the information on the chart to explain why Susan may be wrong.

_____

_____

_____

Test A Booklet

19a

1 mark

19b

1 mark

19c

1 mark

TOTAL

20. Each item below costs the amount shown.

wheelbarrow
£40.80

tape measure
£3.08

wristwatch
£15.50

Work out the cost of:

20a

1 mark

a. Ten tape measures.

20b

1 mark

b. One hundred wristwatches.

20c

1 mark

c. One thousand wheelbarrows.

WORKING
OUT AREA

21. Use a pencil line to map each event to a suitable place on the chance line.

0   1

You will get wet when you
next have a shower.

You will see your teacher on
a normal day at school.

You will get tails when
you next toss a coin.

You will spend Christmas
Day on the moon.

21

1 mark

22. You can use this graph to convert miles into kilometres and kilometres into miles.

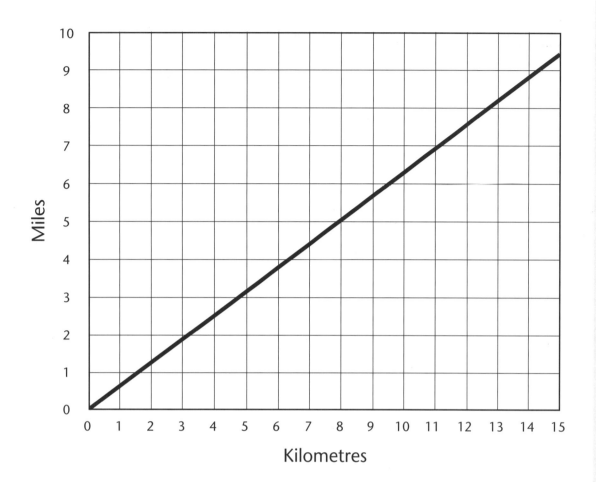

Miles (vertical axis)

Kilometres (horizontal axis)

Use the graph to work out approximate answers to these questions:

a. How many kilometres in 7 miles?

How many miles in 4 kilometres?

22a

1 mark

b. How many kilometres in 4 miles?

22b

1 mark

TOTAL

How many miles in 9 kilometres?

13

Test A
Booklet

23. Three different numbers have a mean of 27.
Two of the numbers are 23 and 36.

What is the third number? Show your working.

WORKING
OUT AREA

23

1 mark

24a. Which is the larger amount,
'two-fifths of 100' or '30% of
50', and by how much?
Show your working.

The larger amount is

_____

by _____

WORKING
OUT AREA

24a

1 mark

b. Which is the smaller amount,
'75% of 120' or 'nine-tenths of
110', and by how much?
Show your working.

The smaller amount is

_____

by _____

WORKING
OUT AREA

24b

1 mark

25. Read the descriptions in the left-hand column and connect each one with a pencil line to a sensible estimate in the right-hand column.

Weight of a jar of jam	11 metres
	25 centimetres
Width of a footpath	450 grams
	10 litres
Length of a bus	110 metres
	10 grams
Capacity of a bucket	1.5 metres
	14 millilitres
Length of a matchbox	7 centimetres
Weight of a pound coin	20 kilograms

25

3 marks

26. Write in the missing digit.

WORKING
OUT AREA

$$\boxed{}\,\boxed{1}\,\boxed{6} \div \boxed{1}\,\boxed{6} = \boxed{2}\,\boxed{6}$$

26

1 mark

TOTAL

STOP HERE

15

Mental Arithmetic Test

CALCULATOR NOT ALLOWED

For this test you will need only a **pencil** or **pen**.
You are **NOT** allowed to use a **scrap piece of paper**, a **ruler**, a **calculator** or an **eraser**.

Marks scored [ ]

Marks possible 20

Listen carefully to the instructions read out
to you at the beginning of the test.

Q Practice question

| cm |

You will have five seconds for each of these questions:

1.		24 53
2.	
3.	
4.	p
5.	

You will have ten seconds for each of these questions:

6.	kg	29 12
7.	£	£10 £3.75
8.	
9.	miles	60 $1\frac{1}{2}$

Q

10.	
11.		63 150
12.	
13.	
14.		7 13 16
15.	£

You will have 15 seconds for each of these questions:

16.		$\frac{4}{5}$ 60
17.		9 8 37
18.	°	73°
19.	£
20.	3 8 18 16 12

19. Award 1 mark each for a–c (do not award the **3** mark for a or b if the £ sign is missing).

a. £300

b. £300

c. Award 1 mark for an explanation which indicates that the amount raised each month has varied, and that the money raised in July may or may not be sufficient to reach the target. (The average amount collected is only £200 per month.)

Use the single bar chart to ask your child more questions about the amount of money raised over the six-month period. Look out for any local fund-raising campaign that might display a similar chart in your area. If you see any, discuss the information shown with your child.

Part c requires your child to give a sound logical reason for his or her answer. This style of question is becoming increasingly popular, and is designed to lead the child to make predictions based on known facts.

20. Award 1 mark each for a–c (answers must **3** show the £ sign).

a. £30.80

b. £1550

c. £40 800

This question is about place value. It tests your child's ability to multiply decimal amounts by 10, 100 or 1000 by shifting the decimal point one, two or three places to the right. Practise this activity with your child when going round the shops: look at the price of something and then multiply it by 10, 100 and 1000.

21. Award 1 mark if all four events are correctly **1** aligned on the chance line (use discretion).

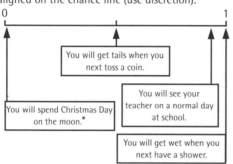

This question involves mathematical 'probability'. You can help to improve your child's understanding of this topic by discussing whether a particular event is certain, very likely, likely, unlikely, very unlikely or impossible. Explain to him or her that probability (also called 'likelihood') is measured on a scale between 0 and 1: a probability of 0 means 'absolutely impossible', and a probability of 1 means 'absolutely certain'. Probability is also sometimes referred to as 'chance', and thus we have expressions such as 'a 1 in 3 chance' or 'a fifty per cent chance'. (*Accept Christmas Day on or just fractionally beyond 0.)

22. Award 1 mark each for a and b if both **2** answers in each part are correct (use discretion).

a. about 11 kilometres   about 2½ miles

b. about 6½ kilometres   about 5¾ miles

Ask your child to convert more distances from miles into kilometres and vice versa, using the graph. Encourage him or her to draw lines on the graph using a pencil and ruler, rather than try to find the answers by eye.

23. Award 1 mark for a correct answer, provided **1** that some relevant working out is shown.
22

Relevant working out could include the following calculations: $27 \times 3 = 81$; $23 + 36 = 59$; $81 - 59 = 22$.

24. Award 1 mark each for a and b, provided that **2** some relevant working out is shown.

a. Two-fifths of 100 is the larger amount, by 25 (do not award a mark unless both parts are correct).

b. 75% of 120 is the smaller amount, by 9 (do not award a mark unless both parts are correct).

Relevant working out for part a could include the following calculations: $100 \div 5 = 20$; $20 \times 2 = 40$; 10% of $50 = 5$; $5 \times 3 = 15$; $40 - 15 = 25$.

Relevant working out for part b could include the following calculations: $75\% = \frac{3}{4}$; $\frac{3}{4}$ of $120 = 90$; $\frac{1}{10}$ of $110 = 11$; $11 \times 9 = 99$; $99 - 90 = 9$.

25. Award 1 mark for any two correct answers, to **3** a maximum of 3 marks.
Weight of a jar of jam – 450 grams
Width of a footpath – 1.5 metres
Length of a bus – 11 metres
Capacity of a bucket – 10 litres
Length of a matchbox – 7 centimetres
Weight of a pound coin – 10 grams

Estimation and approximation are important aspects of the Key Stage 2 maths curriculum, and questions involving these skills often appear in National Test papers. Your child should know the common metric units, be able to convert from one metric unit to another, and be able to make sensible decisions about the best metric unit to use in a given situation. Help your child to practise estimation by asking questions about the height, length and mass of everyday objects.

26. Award 1 mark for a correct answer. **1**
416

Point out that multiplying the known number in the sum by the answer will give the required number.

Parent's Booklet

Answers to Test B

Q   **MARKS**

1. Award 1 mark each for a and b, provided that **2** both answers are correctly given in each (credit answers with the units missing).
   a. 48p
      65g
   b. £358
      £68

2. Award 1 mark for a correctly drawn mirror **1** image:

3. Award 1 mark if both answers are correct. **1**
   06:35   14:55

4. Award 1 mark each for a–d (credit answers **4** with the units missing).
   a. £1.20
   b. 80p
   c. 324 envelopes
   d. 120 envelopes

5. Award 1 mark each for a–c. **3**
   a. The whole table must be filled in correctly to gain 1 mark:

Boys		Girls	
Name	Age	Name	Age
John	11	Sally	11
Edward	10	Katie	11
Sam	11	Jane	10

   b. Stuart's name should be written in the box below Edward in the **Boys** circle.
   c. Jenny's name should be written in the box on the left below Jane, outside both circles.
      (Note that two boxes remain empty.)

6. Award 1 mark each for a and b. **2**
   a. 5250
   b. 37

Tips to help your child – Test B

A **calculator** can be used when answering any of the questions in this test. However, it will not necessarily make all of the questions easier. Part of the skill of using a calculator is knowing **when** to use it.

Make up sets of 'missing number' questions for your child. Use any numbers under 100 and multiples of 5 or 10 above 100. Allow your child to choose his or her method: either using a calculator or using a pencil and paper. Try to emphasize the fact that if you know two numbers in a calculation, you can always find the third by carrying out an appropriate operation with the two numbers that you know.

Your child may at first have trouble in understanding the idea of a 'mirror image'. Allow him or her to practise this activity using squared paper and a variety of shapes.

Invent some more time conversion problems like those in the question. Also help your child to practise changing 24-hour clock times into am and pm times.

This question involves using all four operations (adding, subtracting, multiplying and dividing) in the context of money. Your child could work out the answers using either a pocket calculator or a pencil and paper. The use of a calculator is recommended for parts c and d. Your child will need to keep referring back to the information panel regularly in order to avoid confusion.

Go over the Venn diagram carefully with your child. Explain that John and Sam are in both circles because they are boys who are aged 11. Filling in the table successfully in part a requires your child to understand the information given in the Venn diagram and relate it logically to the information given in the table.

Follow this up by seeing whether your child can now draw a new Venn diagram. Suggest that he or she repeat the two-circle outline, but change the boys' names to girls' names and alter the age criterion.

In parts b and c, your child needs to consider the age and gender of the child mentioned in order to transfer the child's name successfully into the appropriate box on the Venn diagram.

The use of a calculator is strongly recommended for this question.

Let your child practise multiplying and dividing numbers in the hundreds, tens and units range with the aid of a calculator.

7. Award 1 mark for one correct line of symmetry on all four shapes. Several lines of symmetry are possible for the fourth shape. **1**

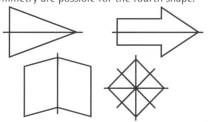

This question is about **reflective symmetry** (also known as **mirror** or **line symmetry**). Tell your child that three of the shapes have only one line of symmetry. (If you put the edge of a mirror along that line, the image in the mirror will complete the original shape exactly.) Encourage your child to try this with a mirror on each of the shapes. He or she will discover that the fourth shape has more than one line of symmetry. Suggest that your child draw some other shapes (such as the capital letters of the alphabet) and try to find their lines of symmetry.

8. Award 1 mark each for a and b. **2**
a. any number between 99 and 104
any number between 106 and 299
any number between 301 and 515
(credit fractional or decimal numbers if appropriate)
b. Award 1 mark if all the numbers are correctly positioned on the number line (use discretion).

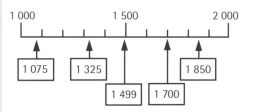

The ability to order a set of numbers is important. Your child needs to understand that the position of a digit within a number affects the value of that digit (for example, the 3 in 370 has a different value from the 3 in 730). Give your child opportunities to arrange groups of numbers in order of size, starting with the largest or smallest. Also, let him or her choose numbers to fill in the gaps between known amounts (as in question 8a).

Question 8b requires your child to **estimate** the positions of some four-digit numbers on a number line. To tackle this successfully your child needs to be able to count and order numbers up to 10 000 or so. Give him or her both oral and written practice in doing this. Comparing the prices of cars in your local newspaper will help to give your child confidence in dealing with these larger numbers in a practical context.

9. Award 1 mark for all three of the following calculations: 2×8 (or 8×2) =16; 16×1 (or 1×16) = 16; 4×4 = 16. **1**

Further problems of this type will give your child valuable practice in recalling times tables and factors. 24, 30, 36 and 40 are all useful numbers to try.

10. Award 1 mark each for a-c. **3**
a. The graph must be complete to gain the mark (use discretion).

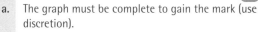
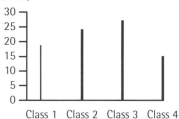

b. Class 3
c. Class 4

This question requires your child to transfer and interpret data. Supplying him or her with squared paper and modifying the table information provided will help to give your child further practice in dealing with this type of problem.

Look out for information given as tables and bar (or line-bar) graphs in magazines, newspapers and breakfast cereal packets. You will also find line or 'trend' graphs which use a line to indicate how something (for example, a patient's temperature) changes over time.

11. Award 1 mark each for a and b. **2**
15
22

The use of a calculator is recommended for this question. For part a, show your child how to find the required number by reversing the operation: 99 + 51 = 150 and 150 ÷ 10 = 15. For part b, point out that the required number can be found by dividing the known number in the sum by the answer to the sum.

12. Award 1 mark each for a and b. **2**
a.

b. 32cm

If your child cannot easily recognize an obtuse angle (more than 90° but less than 180°), encourage him or her to use a protractor for part a of this question. Make sure that your child is also familiar with the names and properties of acute, reflex and right angles. For part b, your child needs to understand the word 'perimeter'.

13. Award 1 mark each for a and b. **2**
a. $23 \times 4 = 92$ **or** $24 \times 4 = 96$
b. 105

For part (a), your child should make a sensible guess as to which numbers multiply by 4 to give a two-digit number starting with 9, then check with a calculator. For part (b), show your child that reversing the operation will provide the required number: $15 \times 7 = 105$.

| Q | Answers | MARKS | Tips |

14. Award 1 mark for each successfully completed row of the table (excluding the first row). **3**

Time in minutes	Tally	Frequency
1–4	IIII	4
5–8	IIII II	7
9–12	IIII	5
13–16	IIII III	8

This is a straightforward task requiring transference and interpretation of data; but dealing with so many numbers requires your child to be particularly careful and accurate when moving the information from the chart to the table. A useful tip is to suggest (if necessary) that your child cross out each journey time on the chart once he or she has recorded it using tally marks on the table. This helps to avoid confusion and errors in the transfer process.

15. Award 1 mark each for a and b. **2**

a.

between five thousand and fifty thousand

more than two hundred thousand

| 1 490 000 | 105 000 | 3706 | 34 700 |

less than five thousand

more than fifty thousand but less than one hundred and fifty thousand

b. 170

Take any opportunities that arise to help your child improve his or her understanding of number values – especially with larger numbers. Invent some number games in a similar style to part a of this question. The answers could be given orally or in writing. Don't always set the problem yourself: let your child set some for you. Other suggestions for activities involving number values can be found in the 'tips' for question 8 and for Test A question 15.

As a follow-up to part b, suggest other numbers and ask how many tens, hundreds or thousands they are equivalent to.

16. Award 1 mark each for a–c. **3**
a. 300 (or three hundred)
b. $\frac{1}{3}$ (or a third or $\frac{100}{300}$)
c. grapes and apples

Although it is possible that your child will work out the correct answers to this question either mentally or using pencil and paper, it is far more efficient to use a calculator in this case.

17. Award 1 mark each for a and b (credit answers without the units). **2**
a. 1744 miles
b. $214\frac{1}{2}$ miles (or 214.5 miles)

A calculator is recommended for this question. To give your child some practice in solving problems of this kind, ask him or her to calculate the distances between various towns and cities in Britain or Europe using the distance charts in a road atlas or travel guide.

18. Award 1 mark each for a and b. **2**
a. $315 \times 39 = 12\ 285$
b. $1296 \div 6 = 216$

For part a, your child should start by calculating that the last digit of the answer must be 5. He or she should then make a sensible guess as to which tens digit is the most likely to produce the answer, and then check his or her hypothesis using a calculator. For part b, point out that the required number can be found by multiplying the answer to the sum by the known number in the sum.

19. Award 1 mark each for a and b if both parts of each are correct. **2**
a. 3.009, 3040
b. 490, 2.036

See the 'tip' for Test A question 11. Point out that the quickest way to convert from one metric unit to another is to move the decimal point an appropriate number of places to the left or right.

20. Award 1 mark each for a–c. **3**
a. 25%
b. $\frac{1}{3}$ (or a third)
c. 36

In order to answer all of the parts of this question, your child will need to have some understanding of angles. Depending on the extent of his or her knowledge, he or she may work out the answers either by pure mathematical calculation or by first using a protractor to measure the angles and then calculating.

21. Award 1 mark each for a–c. **3**
a. 3.49
b. Any of the following combinations of numbers:
400/410/420/430/440/450/460/470/480/490 ÷ 10
= 40/41/42/43/44/45/46/47/48/49
c. 1.2735

A calculator should be used for this question. Part a can be done either by adding 12.91 and 2.34 or by adding 6.48 and 8.77; in either case, the answer should then be subtracted from 18.74. For part b, any digit can be placed in the tens column of the answer; the answer should then be multiplied by 10. For part c, a calculator will definitely be helpful! This task requires your child to take care when keying in decimal points.

Q	Answers	MARKS	Tips

22. Award 1 mark for each pair correctly matched. **2**

y plus y		y minus 4
2y		y – 4

Only attempt to help your child with this question if you have a sound understanding of algebra. Otherwise, you may confuse your child!

23. Award 1 mark for the correct length circled. **1**
4.5m

See the 'tip' for Test A question 25.

24. Award 1 mark if the other three possibilities **1** are **all** correctly identified:
T T H, T T T and H H H (in any order).

To answer this question, your child should approach the problem logically and record the possible outcomes in the form of a structured list.

Answers to Test C

Q		MARKS

1. Award 1 mark each for a and b (do not award **2** the mark if the £ sign is missing).
a. £30
b. £38

2. Award 1 mark each for a–e (award the mark **5** if the unit of measure is missing).
a. $1296cm^2$
b. $216cm^2$
c. $7776cm^3$
d. 3
e. $2592cm^2$

3. Award 1 mark for the correct answer. **1**
3.6
Award an additional mark if the number 12.96 appears in the 'working out area'.

4. Award 1 mark for each correct angle value. **5**
$a = 125°$ $b = 55°$ $c = 69°$ $d = 55°$ $e = 125°$

5. Award 2 marks for all the numbers correctly **2** arranged.
2.202   2.02   2.002   0.22

6. Award 1 mark each for a–c. **3**
a. 15 minutes (award a mark if the unit is missing)
b. any value between 2 and 3 minutes
c. 20mph (do not award a mark if the unit is missing)

7. Award 1 mark for the correct answer. **1**
0.248

8. Award 1 mark for the correct answer. **1**
$\frac{1}{3}$ (credit 1:3 or 1 in 3)

9. Award 1 mark each for a–c. **3**
a. $n = 2$
b. $n = 3$
c. $n = 4$

10. Award 1 mark for the correct answer. **1**
1.334t **or** 1334kg (do not credit an answer without an appropriate unit).

11. Award 1 mark each for a and b (credit **2** answers with the units missing).
a. $143.75m^2$ (accept $143\frac{3}{4}m^2$)
b. $75m^2$

12. Award 1 mark each for a–c. **3**
a. £60 and £15 (in any order)
b. £3.30
c. 3 hours 36 minutes (credit 3.6 hours)

Answers to Mental Arithmetic Test

Q	

p.35 Award 1 mark for each correct answer.
1. 77
2. 8
3. 90
4. 20p
5. 30 084
6. 70kg
7. £6.25
8. 104

9. 90 miles
10. 60
11. 87
12. 700
13. 2.1
14. 12
15. £1.14
16. 48cm
17. 35
18. 107°
19. £7.60
20. 3, 18 and 12 should be circled

INSTRUCTIONS FOR THE MENTAL ARITHMETIC TEST

You will need Test Paper A for your child (the grid for the answers is on page 16) and a clock or a watch that measures accurately in seconds.

Read out the following instructions to your child in a relaxed and friendly manner at the start of the test. Answer any questions that your child might ask.

This test has 20 questions and will only last for about 5 minutes. Each question will be read out to you twice. You must work out the answers to the questions in your head but you can jot things down outside the answer box if this is helpful to you. Make sure you write your answer in the box alongside the correct question number. For some questions, useful information to help your memory is given to you next to the answer box. As you work through the test the questions get harder but you will be allowed more time to work out the answers. If you want to change an answer, put a cross through your first answer and write your second answer next to the answer box. If you find a question too difficult, put a cross in the answer box and wait for the next question to be read

out. You must not ask any questions once the test has started.

Reading out the questions

The questions should be read out to your child in a clear and precise manner and the working out times allowed for each group of questions should be strictly adhered to. It is a good idea to read through the questions beforehand so that when you are asking your child the questions for real your delivery is smooth and confident. Read each question twice allowing only a short pause between each reading. At the start of each timed group of questions tell your child how long they have to work out the answers to that group of questions. The time allowed for each question should begin as soon as you have finished reading the question for the second time. Read out the practice question first and use this as a warm-up for both you and your child. (Don't forget to start your timing as soon as you have read the question for the second time!) Finally, check that your child has written the practice question answer in the correct box on the answer page, answer any further queries your child might have and then begin the test.

MENTAL ARITHMETIC TEST

Read out all questions twice.

PQ What is half of seventy centimetres?

Say: You will have 5 seconds to answer each of these questions.

1. Add together twenty-four and fifty-three.
2. Take seven away from fifteen.
3. Half of a number is forty-five. What is the number?
4. Four people share eighty pence equally between them. How much do they each receive?
5. Write the number thirty thousand and eighty-four in figures.

Say: You will have 10 seconds to answer each of these questions.

6. What is double twenty-nine kilograms add twelve kilograms?
7. Sue bought a book using a ten-pound note and received £3.75 change. What was the cost of the book?
8. How many quarters are there in twenty-six whole ones?
9. A train travels at sixty miles per hour for an hour and a half. How far does it travel?

10. How many five-pence pieces are the same as three pounds?
11. Write the number that is sixty-three less than one hundred and fifty.
12. What is six hundred and ninety-nine to the nearest ten?
13. Find half of four point two.
14. Give the mean of seven, thirteen and sixteen.
15. One packet of biscuits costs thirty-eight pence. How much will three packets cost?

Say: You will have 15 seconds to answer each of these questions.

16. Work out the length that is four-fifths of sixty centimetres.
17. From the product of nine and eight subtract thirty-seven.
18. One angle in a triangle measures seventy-three degrees. What is the sum of the other two angles?
19. Write down the cost of four audiotapes at one pound ninety each.
20. Circle three numbers on your answer sheet that are factors of thirty-six.

Say: The test is over. Put down your pen [or pencil].